A History of Light

for Cary — w. all
the warmth of past +
present meetings

Alvar
3/99

Books by Alvaro Cardona- Hine

Romance de Agapito Cascante, Repertorio Americano, Costa Rica, 1955

The Gathering Wave, Alan Swallow, Denver, 1961

The Flesh of Utopia, Alan Swallow, Denver, 1964

Menashtash, Little Square Review, Santa Barbara, 1969

Agapito, Charles Schribner's Sons, New York, 1969

Spain, Let This Cup Pass From Me, translation of Vallejo's last book,
   Red Hill Press, San Francisco, 1972

Words on Paper, Red Hill Press, San Francisco, 1974

Two Elegies, Red Hill Press, San Francisco, 1976

The Half-Eaten Angel, Nodin Press, Minneapolis, 1981

When I Was a Father, New Rivers Press, Minneapolis, 1982

Miss O'Keeffe, (collaboration) University of New Mexico Press, 1992

Four Poems About Sparrows, Eye Light Press, New Mexico, 1994

A Garden of Sound, Pemmican Press, Seattle, 1996

A History of Light

A Memoir

SHERMAN ASHER Publishing

Cover design Janice St. Marie
Cover art by Alvaro Cardona-Hine
Book design by Judith Rafaela
ISBN 1-890932-00-0
First Edition

Library of Congress Cataloging-in-Publication Data
    A. history of light : a memoir / Alvaro Cardona-Hine.
      p.   cm.
   ISBN 1-890932-01-9 (hardcover : alk. paper). --ISBN 1-890932-00-0 (trade paper : alk. paper)
1. Cardona-Hine, Alvaro--Childhood and youth. 2. Cardona-Hine, Alvaro--Homes and haunts--Costa Rica. 3. Poets. American--20th century--Biography. 4. Costa Rica--Social life and customs.
5. Hispanic Americans--Biography.   I. Title.
PS3505.A655Z465   1997
818' .5409--dc21
[B]   97-27176
                                 CIP

Sherman Asher Publishing
PO Box 2853
Santa Fe, NM 87504

love is a morning of energy

I was sitting on the lowest branch of the tangerine tree recalling how it was I used to play with water, building aqueducts and dams after the first summer rains, when you came by with your eyes. I tried to hurry and remember how I would myself undermine the dams in my desire to see the water wild between the aqueducts but you were already offering me one of those looks I will never forget, and asking if you could join me, wondering if sharing tangerines was fun.

two

I was always sure you'd come by. I always knew that I was only one half of something and that the other half would show up to make me real. I didn't know that the missing part was that which is wanted and for which one burns against all darkness, but I knew you would arrive one day. Your arrival was natural, inevitable. It was blind light; it was the gravity that lets things fall, but fall in love.

three

I go to Maximilian's house, play with his Great Dane, kick the soccer ball a few times, watch Maximilian steal chocolates out of his mother's clothes closet, where she thought they were safe, and none of it engages me. Finally, I have to leave. I do it nonchalantly but it's a leave-taking. I am no longer interested in my former life, the life which seemed so perfect a few weeks ago. And it frightens me, for being with you has taken the place of all the things I used to do and all the friends I had. It's the risk I have to take, this single-mindedness, for with it many things have fallen into place: the reason for birds, for afternoons...

Whatever seemed unfinished once now is undefinable. I had thought God was interested in creating puzzles out of life when He had meant for me to stand in awe of beauty. What an easy thing to feel that is when its messenger stands before me.

four

One day I know that you love me with more than every fiber of your body. The next day it is your turn, while I feel headachy and ill, suffering from an imagined slight, or your absence, or a momentary turning to another as if that other existed or had any power to destroy what we have built over eons of time, making sure that eternity has the freshness of weeks, of a few skinny winter months.

five

That you will die, and I will die, and the sickly peach tree on the side of your castle bloom no more than a few times after, itself in a hurry to join us, we never doubt. We talk about it with our hands, hands sweaty and lemony from holding hands, and otherwise suffering deliciously, in silence, those afternoons when the grownups wisely leave us to our own resources.

six

Since our families live across the street from each other, and our bedroom windows face each other over the tops of the cork trees, you could project your silhouette onto your blinds at night if you wanted to or were careless, and I could sit by my window however long it took waiting to have it happen. But I never saw you undress more than once, when in the one dream I have had of that window, the blondness of your hair was conveyed by its shadow, and the boy's body that was still yours burst upon me with the flash of what doesn't seem to know how to ripen and does, still green.

seven

Because we have come to suspect that time is that expendable material we call *now* and not something subject to end, we have given ourselves license and speak about what it will be like when, after your twelfth birthday comes and you are sent back to Germany—interested as your mother is in your education, without realizing that you'll pine away until it's almost too late and that you'll be brought back (to me) to be made healthy again—what it will be like not to know the anxiety of an imminent separation, with all its dangers: the lack of sunlight when the sun is shining, the little deaths everywhere pretending to know how to bloom, the meals I will refuse until I am anemic and they send for you and you come in one day and stand by the side of the bed. All in white, like a nurse, and golden, like the sun, like a flower.

eight

When it rains and we sit by the window, of what use are words? We are the adventure, the fairy-tale frozen in its tracks, two beings charmed by a sortilege. It rains as if it will never end and we love that, we love everything that comes willingly to stay. We see each other reflected on the window pane, see what we need to see: that we are transparent, superimposed on a world itself transparent. Our eyes are at once the means by which we drink in each other and the flowers across the way, glowing in the rain without thirst, patient and passionate because they have no place to go but our looking since they opened their petals.

nine

When we are in my father's library I show you my bloodline, the spines of the books on which our name appears and you ask if I, too, will fall under the spell of poems and stories to the point where I have to create my own.

Yes, I tell you, I am bound that way, I want to invent what has been dearest to me and relate what will happen when that faint smile forever playing at the corners of your mouth blossoms and reveals the wedding-dress-whiteness of your teeth.

ten

With your kitten, which you allow me to play with, I can go ahead and indulge my hands to the full, touching what is most nearly you. But then, not satisfied with touch, I incite the kitten to scratch me, feeling a perverse pleasure in being wounded, however lightly, by something that you own, that is yours, that behaves the way you dance when you are most still, the way you are apt to go blank with daydreams in the middle of a game.

eleven

I pretend you don't exist but see you suddenly in the middle of the lake, among the swans. Or I go nearly twenty-four hours without seeing you when your face appears in the fountain of holy water in the Church of El Carmen. The anonymous miracle lights up the corners where the confessionals have been soiling the light with the story of sin; the whole church brightens up because you are smiling there on the surface of the water.

I don't need the water now; there is no need for me to cross myself. I leave the church and hurry to your house, knowing that you will have beaten me there, in a rush to appear normal and as if you knew nothing about miracles.

   Your mother sits at the piano and plays Rachmaninoff, the snow melting from her fingers as if she were a Russian birch or better yet, a willow half submerged in an icy stream. You are pleased that I listen close, that I understand, and we know that we will never be able to enjoy music alone, without someone to look to for confirmation.

   Afterwards, in the kitchen, where we have gone to have a cookie and a glass of milk, we pretend that nothing has happened.

thirteen

Your gifts make me laugh: a piece of thread that you pluck from the sleeve of your blouse and hand me, just to test and see if I will throw it away; the pebble that got in your shoe the last time we had races around the block; that piece of coconut taffy you pulled out of your mouth and placed in mine without batting an eyelid, laughing, and which I took for a kiss, the first, the only one.

fourteen

We've grown thinner, taller. That's because the heart with our initials that I carved on the cork tree is now below eye level and still sinking, moving down, perhaps wanting to reach the soil and grow roots. I like the two you's: the one I saw the first day and the thinner, taller one I saw just yesterday; but I can't choose which one I like the more because, when I close my eyes, they merge into one.

fifteen

I like to be alone and I like to be without you because then I get to want to be with you. When I am with you I am not thinking, I am in a fog; it's almost as if the time was wasted by my not being my usual self.

Tomorrow I am going to tell you that I like being alone and not tell you why. You'll blanch; I know I'll have been cruel but I won't be able to help myself because afterwards my cruelty will make me love you more. It will also test you.

sixteen

No more tests! Forgive me! Let me explain why I said it. I am not stupid, it's that I think too much. I like to be alone and I like to be without you because then I get to want what I want, and that is to be with you.

You forgive me immediately and then decide that you've been too easy so you're angry again. It's like one of those days of sunlight and mist when even the streets one knows feel untried, unreal, unearthly.

seventeen

The Spanish you speak, as if you lisped ever so little, and as if your R's were too much to ask, that's the best Spanish I've ever heard. I wish you could speak ten times as much, I wish you chattered like most girls do so I could hear Spanish like a river that has overflowed its banks and swallowed everything in its path. But of course you don't speak. You are embarrassed. You think that just because one time I laughed at how you said something I don't like to hear you speak. Listen, first of all, I laughed because I loved what you had done to the language and, second, because I always like to hear you speak. I like the sound of your voice. I like it so much sometimes I don't get to hear what you are saying. When you speak I don't need anything else, neither the silence I used to prize above all else nor the sense you make when I do hear you.

❦

eighteen

Neither of us wants to be married, ever. We talk of our lives as adults with disinterest, as if we hadn't meant and weren't bound to be together for the rest of our lives. So we talk about wanting nobody, wounding each other into thinking we don't want each other.

I know why we do it. We do it because it is another way of saying we don't want anything to change: we want to remain friends forever, this word *friend* being as much as we dare define what we know to be so much no single word or bunch of words could encompass it.

nineteen

After pushing you on the swing and having you push me, I come home still feeling the pressure of your hands on my back. The feeling remains: that you are still pushing me and that I am swinging high enough to reach the loquats by the fence. When I wake up the next morning I have two points of discomfort on my back; my shirt feels funny when I put it on, as if it didn't fit any more. When we meet in the afternoon, we stand amazed before each other: I am amazed because enormous wings have sprouted from your back and you're amazed because something like that has happened to me too.

"Who needs swings now?" I say.

"We do," you reply, "we do, because we can fly off and return when six months have gone by backwards, in that way having to get to know each other all over again and knowing that the swing will hurl us back when we get to today, with my innocent suggestion that we go try my brother's new toy."

❧

twenty

Sometimes your eyes are blue, sometimes green. When they are blue I read you stories about stars finding their way home with the help of sailors. When your eyes turn green, as they are wont to do with the ambition of desire, I switch to tales of the moon lost in the jungle. When your eyes are blue I swim in them like seen questions; when they turn green I look for you among the pines of Europe, trudging through the snow, shoving trolls and mushrooms aside.

When your eyes are blue I match them with madness: I leave you suddenly, without saying goodbye. When they are green I stay until your mother, with that smile she uses to forgive me, has to usher me out of your house.

twenty-one

When one of your braids came apart you laughingly let me try to weave it back into some kind of order. So there I was, three streams of gold in my hands, weaving, weaving. I didn't want it to end. And I wanted to pretend that it was nothing, that you are an ordinary mortal whose hair had to be quickly rearranged so that we could go on with our games. So I told you a ghost story. It mesmerized you as I knew it would, so that I am still weaving, weaving and talking.

What a lucky ghost, to depend for life on being woven into my love's rays, that sunlight that streams from your head.

twenty-two

It is dark now. But I come home illuminated from being with you. I could talk to my family about how I save them electricity—I glow so—but instead of trying to convince them of that I go to my room to eat chocolates. I eat chocolates because you like them. I eat them humming a tune I heard you singing the other day, a song about a miller, a girl with wooden shoes, and the devil who they turned inside out by doing something for which you suddenly blushed and would sing no more.

twenty-three

Your fingernails, little as they are, have small white moons sailing over their crests. And your face has freckles, as if it had lain a whole night exposed to the elements and your skin had photographed the stars. But best of all, when we were whispering so that your little brother would not hear us, my lips accidentally brushed against your neck and went numb. It is as if you had the power to paralyze me, as if I were one of those plants that shrivel up the minute you touch them.

twenty-four

Our two mothers meet for the first time, accidentally, in the street, and they are very polite to each other. I am sure they know already. They would have been polite anyway but they are also very careful and don't talk about us. It is as if the only two people in the world that raise unicorns were to meet and not talk about unicorns.

Your mother is afraid that you will want to stay in Costa Rica. My mother worries that if I lose you I will leave home and never come back, looking for another girl like you.

twenty-five

I haven't told any of my friends at school but they know something is different. I never go with them to the river in the afternoons, I don't invite them over any more. They don't ask, but if they did, I wouldn't tell them anyway. It is only because my life is secret that I feel so good, as if I were a new and mysterious river to myself, a river at whose banks I can sit and watch the water of what you are flow by hour after hour.

twenty-six

I love to make you laugh because when you laugh it is catching. First, the honeysuckle vine starts to laugh, the laughing climbs the wall and spills over the neighbor's roof, already turned to perfume. The roof laughs with sunlight. That makes the sky laugh. The clouds begin laughing and the birds, the whole world is laughing. I look at your eyes and see them reflecting the laughter of the stars.

twenty-seven

Another cruel game: I invent the kind of person I would fall in love with. She's short, has dark hair and dark eyes and only plays with girls. You tell me that you like blond boys with blue eyes, that they must be a foot taller than you and be ten times more intelligent than anyone you know. When we are through we don't know how to repair the damage so we have a few days of uncertainty. I'll call it agony. And it doesn't help to know that I can't ever tell you that I love you because sometimes, sometimes I think that you'd laugh, that I am only a neighbor boy with whom you like to spend your afternoons rehearsing for when you meet that tall blond boy who knows ten times what I know.

twenty-eight

A scary game: we decided to look into each other's eyes and not stop. Of course, it's impossible, but we tried and tried again. At first one is afraid that every thought in one's mind can be read as in an open book. No sooner does one shrug that fear off than one goes past the strange structure of the eye, beyond the pool of blue, into thoughts, real thoughts projected there. But whose thoughts are they? Yours? Mine? They must be mine. So much I want couldn't be coming from you.

twenty-nine

In my house you act even wilder than at yours, with more abandon, as if you belonged there. Whereas when I am at your place I try to remember every rule of politeness instilled into me. It's not that we are that different, it's that the world is yours, you'll never have to worry about it, while with me whatever world there is begins with nothing and ends at my door.

The day you came through my door, my own private door, wearing the furiously white light of your certainty, I had no need for more world, all the world I ever wanted to taste I would taste through you.

thirty

I want to steal your gardenias, the little snails that think to climb your walls, the pebbles in your driveway, even the ones cracked in half by old age. I want that small bear that has lain on its side for two weeks now in a corner of your room, and that impossibly lucky ribbon tied around your hair. Most of all I want that photograph of you that your mother has by her easy chair and which she never looks at, the photograph in which the slightest question in your eyes is offset by a smile about to form on your lips; yes, the one in which you look me straight in the eye, the one after which how could I ever be a thief?

thirty-one

The first time I saw you, when you either didn't see me or pretended you hadn't because...who was I? I thought my eyes had made a mistake so, like a boob, I had to look again and stare. That day, that moment when I stopped being the old me, the kid brought up in the mountains, let me tell you what it felt like: like a killing sword, like electricity, like ammonia, like passing out, like shouting in pools of blood, like no air, like fear of animals, like insanity, like boiling water, like rushing trains, like a ghost in a dark house, like falling in dreams, like falling from a tree, like holding ice against the skin, like wanting water with the heart of a burning lion.

thirty-two

But it was so natural how you did it. It was about two weeks after your family moved into that three-storied brick house across from ours, the one I call the castle, and a few days after I had first seen you, that our doorbell rang and there you were, asking my mother if I could come out to play. My mother turned to me with a funny little smile as if saying, well, this is better than those muddied pals of yours you try to drag in here some of the time, but I was so stunned by my luck at you being the way you are, and by my guilt, for I already loved you, that I couldn't say a word. And what was worse than that, I couldn't move.

thirty-three

So we went to play. I pretended I was unsure, for my mother's benefit, and because that way I could disguise my fright. It fooled no one. You grabbed my hand as only a foreign girl totally unfamiliar with life here in San Jose would have done, and dragged me over to your house. You showed me a huge empty chest, you made me crawl into it then you crawled in yourself and lowered the lid. There we were in the dark, crowded next to each other, not saying a word till you burst out laughing and asked me if I liked it. Of course I liked it. It was the best darkness I'll ever know.

thirty-four

And give me, too, not only your hand that can, after all, hold other things, but your heart even if it has room for others. Not only your hand and heart but your soul which can't be given. And your eyes and your lips.

Notice that I haven't mentioned your name. What is your name? Is it a name like anyone else's, a name one can bandy about, or is it a name one can't pronounce, a name not so foreign as so beautiful that one tastes it on one's lips without uttering it or utters it only as a thought is uttered when it's only a thought?

thirty-six

The back wall of your garden is made up of a row of cypresses where all the spare sparrows in the world are housed. They are guys who failed music school, you say, and we climb the pine tree that faces the cypresses like a sergeant.

Half way up the tree are a group of branches which, maimed in their infancy, grew about each other. We sit there comfortably, without having to hold on with our hands. It is a natural tree house which we go to when we have something particularly stressful to discuss.

Today we do. We know it without having to open our mouths. It is time we said the words we have wanted to hear, the words burning our lips. And we get up the tree only to find that it's only our eyes that can say them. Once again only the eyes. But this time oh so clearly, and knowing that the words have been left far behind, that they are not for us, bonded in that silence as we are.

thirty-seven

At your brother's birthday party, with some twenty youngsters present, we attempt to dance. The music is playing and the adults are anxious to see us pretend we are older than we are. Of course, the others, the kids, are monkeying around to the strains of the waltz but we understand this magnificent chance to hold each other.

Your proximity is so unnerving that I can't listen to your instructions; my feet go any which way. And you try to explain things because it is the perfect cover-up for what you yourself are feeling, whirling about so that your hair whips around and brushes against my cheek. Meantime, frightened as I am, the arm I have around your waist wants to pull you closer so that you can feel this me that your legs have aroused.

thirty-eight

In the veranda, afterwards, we sip the watered-down wine we got instead of lemonade. You keep smiling, trying to reassure me that everything is all right, that you wanted that. The sun, reflecting off the library windows, bathes you in such a soft glow that if you were to disappear, I would know where to find you: you'd be in front of me, made up entirely of light.

thirty-nine

You have chosen the color blue: a blue ribbon, a rhinestone, nothing very much, sometimes merely your eyes or your hair, for after looking at it and closing my eyes, it turns blue. To go along with this color of distance, there is the indescribably absent odor of your body, a perfume which by its absence brings me clean out of myself: I search for you, for the smell of sunshine, of the smile which is the color of your intelligence. What confirms you is whatever blue you have allowed the sky to borrow and the breezes to take to the distant, the offended gardenias, which have committed the sin of not knowing when to stop.

forty

Happy birthday to knowing you two months, three. It's in this way that I learn who you are, with time saying: eat, play, sleep, time saying how your uncle wears nothing but leather pants six thousand miles away, time describing your face to my eyes. It's all time, that's how it happens. But even truer than that would be to say that I knew everything there was to know about you the first time I laid eyes upon you. Everything since has been a confirmation, a sign of great accuracy and a little rubber band holding hard to a bouquet of flowers.

forty-one

I bring you some flowers, weeds actually, that have bloomed in the empty lots behind my house, and you receive them with the economy of surprise that points toward womanhood. They go into a jar and you add water, but in half an hour they have collectively dropped and hung their heads in death's shame. So the next day I trek across town to the florist who is my father's best friend and get him to give me a rose, a maroon rose that knows no dying and which you receive with the exuberance of a child.

forty-two

Instead of dying, we'll invent a new way to disappear from the world. We will find the perfect way to breathe so that we will begin to vibrate unobtrusively and slowly turn into invisible entities, go to another location in a different, higher guise. As we are doing it, chunks of our bodies will break off and float away, effortlessly, painlessly. It will be an ecstasy to let go of ourselves, of bodies which can only do five things at a time. What I want is another life in a universe in which you are everything, and in which I have to discover that fact slowly, surely, with a joy of recognition that will make my present happiness nothing by comparison.

forty-three

I arrive and you're not there. I pace up and down your courtyard, right the turtle your brother had left upside down and feel the sadness, the emptiness. The cook says you've all gone to the country for the day and won't be back till night time. It gives me a chance to look at the things we play with without you. Let me tell you, they are strange. The swing hangs there suspended from the high *jacaranda* branch as if the merest touch wouldn't set it in motion. Your skates, in a corner, one of them on its side, would go by any other name one chose to give them. And the patch of earth under the library windows, where we found the dead sparrow last week, has erupted as with a childhood disease. Yes, our beans have sprouted and one swollen yellow seed has a small clod of dirt for a hat. Nothing moves, though. Everything is frozen, waiting for you to come wind it into life. This includes me.

forty-four

I kidnap you. You're not supposed to leave the block but I take you to the entrance of the zoo, a few blocks up, by Maximilian's house, so you can see where I used to think of myself as Tarzan, king of the apes. It's very dark there because the trees are enormous. And the ground tips over and rushes pell-mell down to the river. At the river we are going to build a raft and sail down-stream. But you balk. What scares you is the rustle from within the bamboo thicket, and the snake that pokes its head out and flicks its tongue at you. I should be firm, use force: look how easy it is for you to make me do anything you want, even play house, something for which I would have to pay dearly if my friends found out.

"Don't you want to be alone with me in the world?"
"Yes."
"Well, then?"
"I don't like snakes."
"They can't harm you."
"Yes they can. They are ugly."
"That one was beautiful."

"Beautiful!"

"Yes, beautiful."

"Beautiful like I am beautiful?"

You are daring me to say that I think you are. But I am supposed to be a boy, and one who has just described a snake as beautiful, so I don't say it. Later, at your house, where two cups of hot chocolate are waiting for us, with the milk beginning to form a film at the top, I say it, more into the cup than not.

"You're beautiful."

Your eyes, on the other side of your chocolate cup, look at me through a film of pleasure and pain.

forty-five

It's as if, after asking for it, you didn't want to hear it; as if, knowing you have to be a woman who will use her beauty to advantage, you wanted to cleave to a state in which there was no trace of vanity.

Meantime, you don't know how wonderful it feels to have said it, to have dared bring to life in you a glimmer of what I feel. I haven't told you I love you, true; that I can't ever bring myself to utter, but I have said it nonetheless because by saying you are beautiful I have uttered its corollary, what everyone knows but never admits, that we always fall in love with what is beautiful, that we can't help it.

forty-six

Thoughtlessly, you ask me into your room. On your bed, laid out in an incredible array of feminine certainty, are your new clothes, the ones you will wear when you sail to Germany. One is a white dress made out of stuff as light as beaten egg white. You dazzle me with your white blouses, your matching suits, because with those clothes you are not only able to sail away but are happy to do so and you are no longer here, where if you were, you'd have seen the initial confusion in my eyes and then the pain.

And now, a moment later, now that you have returned, you do see and hurriedly take me out of your room and attempt to talk about the unspoken Jehovah things we would never have to have talked about if you hadn't already left me.

forty-seven

So it means crowding all of life, all of many endless years, into nine days. Nine days that will never pass. Or that will pass, I am not exaggerating, as if they were an entire lifetime.

My father, who is always reading the most wonderful books, tells of a man , an opium addict who, under the effect of the drug, lived an entire lifetime in a single evening, a life with all the tedium, the awakening, the fire, the surprises, disappointments and fulfillments that take place in sixty or eighty years.

I want to ask him what opium is just to see if he says that it's you.

forty-eight

As if to prove what I say, your trip has been postponed one or two weeks, nobody's sure, but a ship at harbor in Puerto Limon, in need of repairs.

Your mother lets you wear your new white dress so our happiness is complete. You never wanted to leave: it was the dress that had lured you into wanting to depart, as if it had a life of its own where the only thing that counted was its passage through the world.

To celebrate, we lie on the grass looking at the sun through closed eyelids and then through our closed fingers. We are trying to erase the world, that little piece of sadness, and float down a river championed by permanence, like butterflies.

forty-nine

But one narrows down to be river, one opens up to be ocean. I know where you are going. I, too, shall go one day, fly away to mountains of ice and larch. I won't even be looking for you, you'll be my eyes. And I will be dressed in the clothes that demand passage.

It is only now, when we wear no mask whatsoever, that love can have that unpossessed angry heat of childhood in the sunlight.

fifty

It is close to nighttime. Only one star, Venus, shines in the West, and it is bright enough to cast my shadow, shadow I give the name of crow. When I flap my arms up and down the crow flies to your window, which is wet with light.

I don't know whether he pecks on the glass or not but in any case you come to the window, you open it and look at the star. And then at me, without my shadow. Everything is ending.

fifty-one

You in my mind, your name in my tongue, that's what gets interrupted by everything but you. Knowledge of you is vast and complex: you are the earthquake and I am the passion fruit vine with all my flowers shaking like bells. You are the bee going from one to another of flowers which, like my brain cells, do nothing but produce honey for you, for the you that is always here, brushing aside petals and pistils.

fifty-two

When you ask me if I have ever loved anyone I play it safe and tell you about the girl with the long curls I knew four years ago. Do eight-year-olds fall in love? Sure they do. And they fall out of love merely by being teased about it, as I was. I was teased by an older cousin and was so angry I wept. After that I couldn't go out to the street and play games for a while. It was all right, falling out of love allowed me to remember the one time I was in her house and the house smelled stale.

Obliquely, so as to let you know how much I love you, I begin describing the smells in your castle. The kitchen is impossible to describe, its odors depend on a cook's whim. But the dining room smells of bread and oak, of chocolate, wine and wax. The library smells like the back of a quiet clock, opened up to reveal its gears. The living room is sure to smell of voices and piano strings, and the whole upstairs, including your bedroom, smells like those shy vine roses one finds unattended in the garden of blind people, wind-fresh, like a song one never thought of singing.

fifty-three

Your brother is *it* and the two of us hide behind the heavy curtains in the dining room. And to show me how excited you are, how wonderful it is to be a hunted animal, you place my hand over your heart. I feel it beating, beating, like whatever lies at the very center of the earth, of the universe.

And maybe your brother will be called by a grown-up for some reason, forget the game he's playing, and leave us here behind these curtains, my hand on your heart, for as long as it takes.

fifty-four

We manage to climb the stuffy cork tree by my house, thick with foliage and dust, and discover an old bird's nest. Looking carefully, we see a few downy feathers, small and grey-blue, at the bottom, almost as if a rainbow was trying to gain a foothold there.

Back at your house, your mother is not upset that you come in all dusty and disheveled; she seems to agree with us that the world is meant to be explored and she knows that you are about to spill over into a life in which everything natural is *verboten*. How she can reconcile the two things is a mystery.

fifty-five

Your forehead is that great place beneath a tree where one may sit to dream and get altogether lost in it. The day for this must have the sunshine of your hair. And I know what your laughter turns into: water. Water so free and so humble all at once. Beyond that water lies your voice, ready with the thoughts of your forehead.

At the river, half a mile from the Zoo, there is a rock that I compare with your forehead. It juts out of the hill, above the water. When I am a better swimmer I want to leap from it and sail past your eyes like a bird.

fifty-six

You are now on that boat that could not remain unfixed and has sailed away. I imagine standing by your side looking at the horizon, and it couldn't be more empty. You say it will be like this for days and days, grey and silent, and I want to ask you why when I realize that I am not there, that here the sun is shining and that across the street a voice is singing, the voice of a girl I knew in the voice of a mother. How wonderful, I tell myself, how wonderful that she can sing like that when you're not there. Or that you can sing like that from so far, so far away.

These pages were written in the early 80's when I lived in Minnesota, teaching poetry in the schools.

One winter Sunday I drove three hours through a blizzard to a little town in southern Minnesota called Canton, just beyond another one called Harmony. By the time I got there the town was snowbound and I lived that week going and coming between the school where I taught for a few hours and a motel room as nondescript as a dead fly. In order not to fall prey to the television I began to recall things out of my childhood, looking for a poem or something maybe even larger. Suddenly, there *she* was, this apparition from the Thirties.

This is how the book began, thanks to a blond German girl. It tumbled out. In five days all white with tons of snow the book wrote itself, so effortlessly I had to change nothing, not even the names I felt incumbent to leave out so that those who read the story can supply their own, out of their own unsullied past.

ABOUT THE AUTHOR:

Alvaro Cardona-Hine, writer, painter, and composer, was born in Costa Rica in 1926 and came to the United States when he was thirteen years old. His work has been published in thirteen books of poetry, prose, and translation, and appeared in over sixty literary and national journals and numerous anthologies. He has been the recipient of an NEA grant, a Bush Foundation Fellowship and a Minnesota State Arts Board grant. He makes his living as a painter, selling his work from a small gallery in the mountain village of Truchas, New Mexico. His musical compositions and texts have been performed internationally. He is currently at work on an opera.

ABOUT THE PRESS

Sherman Asher Publishing, an independent press established in 1994, is dedicated to changing the world one book at a time. You can play a role by supporting poetry and fine literature—attend readings, volunteer in the schools, read to your children, and give yourself the gift of poetry.

COLOPHON:

The cover and title pages are type set in Adobe Weiss®
and Fontek Bickley Script. The body copy is type set in
Adobe Chaparral™, a new type face designed by Carol
Twombly inspired by a 16th century manuscript. The pages
are adorned by Adobe Wood Type Ornaments.

This book was printed in the United States of America
by Vaughn Printing on acid free paper.